Kim-
STAY
STRONG!

Steve

STEVE DIGGS

PART OF THE SERIES
FAST-FORWARD LEADERSHIP

Get the

"GREEN LIGHT"

SELL MORE. CLOSE MORE.
EARN MORE. HAVE MORE FUN.

BOYD &
FRANKLIN
PUBLISHERS

A **14 DAY PLAN** THAT WILL
REVOLUTIONIZE YOUR SELLING CAREER

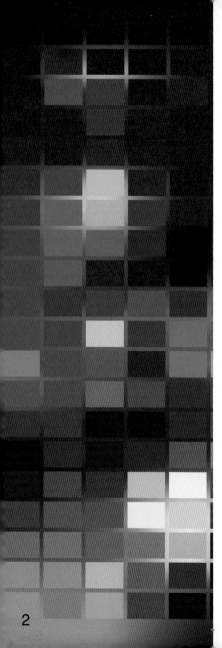

ISBN: 978-0-9909009-1-7

Book Layout Inhaus Creative, Nashville (www.inhauscreative.com)
Printed and bound in China.

Visit Steve at www.SteveDiggs.com

BOYD &
FRANKLIN
PUBLISHERS

CONTENTS:

INTRODUCTION

The truth is, being a salesperson is nothing new for you. As a matter of fact, you've been a salesperson all your life…and you will be for the rest of your life. It's sort of a womb to the tomb thing.

Think about it. From the day you were hatched, you were selling. When you were hungry, sleepy, or poopy…you had to sell Mom on feeding you, putting you to bed, or cleaning and changing you, right? So, how did you do it? You cried. And, if that didn't work, you cried harder…and harder… and harder. Think of those crying spells as your first efforts to close a sale.

By the time you were three, your skills had expanded. By then you were asking for everything from a second dessert to a candy bar at the checkout.

Within a few years you'd become a pretty sophisticated negotiator. You'd learned that, if you wanted something, you probably had to make a case for it. At first, you simply pleaded. But then you learned to trade. Those were the days when you offered to trade your PB&J sandwich for Erin's chocolate cake.

By your later teens, especially if you're a guy, you were learning that guys who got dates were the best salesmen. They dressed correctly. They had a good self-image and wowed with their presentations. They proved to be perfect gentlemen. (On a related topic: Have you ever wondered why the worst-looking dudes seem to end up with the best-looking girls? But, I digress.)

4

I realize that most of you reading this book are no longer amateur salespeople. At some point you learned that you could actually monetize these skills. So you decided to make a career of it. You've gone from crying, begging, and trying to impress the opposite sex to asking for orders.

This book is designed to help those of you who are in a hurry to suck up some really effective ideas that you can begin using tomorrow to sell more stuff.

MY 6 PROMISES: If you will read, internalize, and apply the upcoming 14 Thought Sparklers…your sales career will be revolutionized.

1. You will close more deals.
2. You will advance further.
3. You will help other people live better lives.
4. You will earn a fabulous income.
5. You will wake to the morning with a truly optimistic attitude.
6. And, at the end of the road…you will look over your shoulder at where you've been with a smile.

So, What Gives Me the Right to Write this Book?

Frankly, I don't read books by authors who aren't experts in their field. Neither should you. Not to be immodest, but I am a great salesman. **I'm average at most things** and terrible at some. **But when it comes to selling…I know how to do.** Over the decades I've sold many millions of dollars of products and services. I've trained some great salespeople. And, I believe, I've helped a lot of people in the process.

I began my professional sales career around age four. I'd found that there was a certain type of red clay under our home that could be shaped, molded, and dried into cool little bowls. I enjoyed making and painting said bowls and presenting them to my mom who was always effusive with her praise. Bolstered by Mom and driven by a desire to earn some money, one day I launched out into our neighborhood selling my painted bowls to the neighbors. Out of pity (or a desire to get rid of the local Dennis the Menace), the neighbors shelled out and I began to make sales. Of course Mom was mortified.

Mom's growing awareness that I actually liked selling (along with a desire not to be the neighborhood joke) led her to help me find more suitable wares to peddle. We found ads in my comic books for industrious kids who wanted to sell greeting cards. I was off and running! Soon I was selling

everything: flower seeds, fire extinguishers, Christmas wreaths, and Swipe cleaning detergent. And I was really making money and winning accolades!

At 17, upon high school graduation, I went to work for the famous Southwestern Company in Nashville. Each summer they sent hundreds of college students all over the country selling books door-to-door. After an eye-opening, one-week sales school, I was dispatched to South Georgia. It was a tough summer. At first, I was stationed out in the county where some of the houses were hundreds of yards apart and temperatures regularly exceeded 100 degrees...and I had no car. Many of the guys quit within the first few days. The company expected us to hit our first door by 8:00 a.m. and our last at 10:00 p.m....six days a week. But I stuck it out. By the end of the summer I'd

learned a lot about selling—and a lot about me. I ended up on the Top 50 List among the new sales-men. I knew I had learned a skill that would prevent me from ever being unemployed again. I was in charge of my own destiny! It was the most important summer of my life.

Arriving at college in the fall, I determined not to let school get in the way of a good education. Over the next four years I start-ed a number of businesses in my dorm room. After graduation, I went into the real estate business in Nashville. Within less than two years I was in the top four percent of all Middle Tennessee Realtors. From there I went into the car business, where I found myself a top salesman within the first six months.

From there, I opened The Frank-lin Group, Inc. This advertising agency and broadcast production firm would become my professional focus for 25 years. I ran the business on a simple philosophy that "advertising is nothing more than salesmanship to the masses." During its run we helped scores of clients. We never had a cash flow problem. We never had a layoff. And, we never had a money-losing year.

Here's the point: I'm not a terribly smart guy. I don't have the best pedigree. I don't hold any advanced degrees. But the ability to sell has given my family a wonderful lifestyle and level of freedom that is only experienced by a precious few.

You can do this too!

My purpose for this book is to show you how to do the same.

My mission between these pages is threefold:

1 To make you proud of your chosen career.

2 To give you some powerful strategies and effective takeaways that you can begin using immediately.

3 And to leave you so motivated that you can't wait to make your next call!

Now, let's get down to it!

COMING ATTRACTIONS

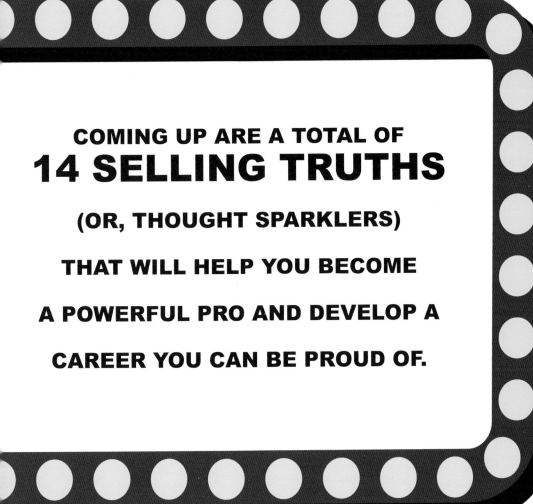

COMING UP ARE A TOTAL OF

14 SELLING TRUTHS

(OR, THOUGHT SPARKLERS)

THAT WILL HELP YOU BECOME

A POWERFUL PRO AND DEVELOP A

CAREER YOU CAN BE PROUD OF.

THOUGHT SPARKLER 1

THE 3 STAGES OF A SALESPERSON'S CAREER

An old sage once remarked,

"A mind once stretched by a **NEW** idea will never return to its original dimension."

I don't expect you to necessarily agree with every assumption, comment, or strategy I share in this book. That's okay. My simple hope is that you will find a few golden nuggets that will revolutionize your selling career.

To begin, selling is about much more than getting appointments, doing demos, pre-closing, and closing. Selling is a profession that today's world cannot survive without. In fact, nothing happens until someone sells something. And, the great thing about being a salesperson is that you will be paid every day exactly what you are worth…not a penny more…not a penny less.

Salespeople who really go the distance go through several phases. I call them

"The 3 Stages of a Salesperson's Life™."

STAGE ONE
The "You Don't Want to Buy This, Do You?" Stage

This is the stage where many potentially great salespeople wash out before they even begin. The great enemy of a young salesperson is the fear of rejection.

The fact is, some people won't need or want your product...whatever it is! Don't confuse the rejection of your product with a rejection of yourself. You and the product, or service you're selling, are two radically different things. Lots of people will reject your product because they don't need, don't want, or don't understand how it will benefit them. The only one of these three things that you can control is the last. This is why you shouldn't wear your feelings on your sleeve, and why you should constantly improve your presentation skills.

STAGE ONE is the time when you should be developing your sales skills. This is when you learn how to deal with objections. This is the stage in your life when you don't have a lot of selling smarts...but you have the luxury of time in which to develop those selling smarts. At this point it's a numbers game. Your primary job is to make lots and lots of presentations. With each presentation you will become better. But remember, even bad presentations (when you make enough of them) will result in some sales. No, your closing ratio won't be very high, but with enough demos you'll still hit the numbers. As they say, even a blind hog will find plenty of acorns if he roots around long enough.

STAGE TWO "THE FRUIT SALAD" STAGE

In the military, some generals become known as "fruit salad" generals. Fruit salad is the name given to the chest full of ribbons and medals that some military leaders wear. Curiously, over the decades, many of America's greatest generals have eschewed wearing all of their medals. Great generals like Dwight Eisenhower and Ulysses Grant rarely wore all the medals they had earned. Other generals, often of far less status, tended to wear everything they had received.

Salesperson beware! "The Fruit Salad" Stage is the most dangerous of all. This is when you've signed a few deals. You're starting to have some self-confidence. People in the office have patted you on the back. You've won a couple of awards. And arrogance begins to set in.

This is the moment to strive for modesty. Remember that you are where you're at because others have invested time and talents helping you succeed. If you've learned anything worthwhile, share it with others and pass it forward. I love the words of the Apostle Paul, who said, "Take heed when you stand, lest you fall."

STAGE

3

18

"THE POWERFUL PRO" STAGE

This is the most glorious and gratifying stage of the three.

THIS IS WHERE THE STAR SALESPEOPLE LIVE.

The Powerful Pro is the salesperson who has learned to lead a balanced and centered life. She sees her life holistically. Making sales and earning an income are important...but they aren't the most important parts of life.

These are the people who are the most focused on their clients' needs. They don't sell stuff that other people don't need. They tailor every presentation to each prospect's individual needs.

Believe me, a client can always tell when there are dollar signs in the salesperson's eyes. People can tell when you want the sale for yourself more than you want the sale to fill a need in the client's life.

The Powerful Pro is the salesperson who won't have to pay his pallbearers to bury him.

STEVE'S TIMELY REMINDERS

There are **2** Leadership Models:

POWER-DRIVEN Leadership

& MENTORING.

The FIRST is usually BAD. But

Mentoring...is a unique type of

leadership that comes up beside another

and **SHOWS...but NEVER SHOVES!**

THE LIKEABILITY FACTOR

FACT: People don't buy stuff from people they don't like. This is a simple-to-understand, concept. Sometimes it's under appreciated. However, this is the most fundamental of all our Thought Sparklers.

At its core, **selling is communication and persuasion**. To accomplish this, we must be likeable people. This means that you don't have the luxury of bringing your problems to work with you. When you arrive at work, everything else goes away. You put on your game face. You focus on your customers and clients. Your only reason for existence is to serve…not to be served.

In my work as a professional speaker I fly in airplanes a lot…over 100 times yearly. On occasion I have heard flight attendants complaining about their jobs and their work conditions. This is stupid, thoughtless, and counterproductive. Their complaining doesn't solve any problems. It puts them in a worse mood. And the worse their mood, the worse the passengers' moods will be. Then, the harder those same flight attendants will have to work to keep those passengers satisfied. A vicious cycle!

I suppose flight attendants can get away with this, because their pay isn't based on commissions. But yours is. As a salesperson, you will make more sales if you are a positive, upbeat human being. I'm not talking about being phony. I'm suggesting that you treat your customers as you would want them to treat you. (This will be a reoccurring theme in this book.)

This means that you should strive to be **LIKEABLE**. Get into your client's shoes. Learn what's on his mind. Find out what motivates (and demotivates) him. Talk to him about what he considers important.

Actually this is pretty simple stuff. **Being likeable requires only three things:**

1) BE A NICE PERSON. Go out of your way to be kind. If your client likes football…talk football. If she is proud of her kids…never fail to ask about them…by name. If your customer likes desserts…show up with a slice of strawberry pie.

2) BE HONORABLE. Do exactly what you say you will do. Don't promise to show a house that you can't arrange to get in. Don't infer that the price is less than it will be. Don't overpromise.

3) SMILE. You don't have to be smart, educated, or pretty to smile. This may be the most important thing you can do.

STEVE'S **TIMELY** REMINDERS

Snooze Alarms are for

LOSERS!

NEVER START A NEW DAY **by breaking**

the last promise you made

To Yourself Last Night.

THOUGHT SPARKLER 3

BECOME MENTALLY AMBIDEXTROUS™

In several of my previous books I've discussed a concept that I call Becoming Mentally Ambidextrous™. But in case you've not read those other writings, I want to share it with you here. This is one of the most important skillsets I've ever learned. It has helped me communicate and persuade people who think very differently than I think. It has helped me get out of myself and touch the hearts of others in effective ways.

When you were in the second grade you may have noticed that one child in the class could write with either his left or his right hand. You called that child ambidextrous.

In much the same way, professional salespeople need to become what I call, Mentally Ambidextrous.

Our brains are divided into two lobes: the right brain and the left brain. It is believed that most people operate primarily from one or the other of the two sides.

Those people who function from their right brains tend to be the folks who are the most relational. They include the creative people in a culture: the artists, the writers, and the musicians. Right-brain people like the process and tend to be people people...and not overly focused on the bottom line.

On the other hand, left-brain people are the analysts. They tend to be the accountants and the engineers in a culture. They focus on the bottom line.

To be a successful salesperson, you need to understand that **you don't have the luxury of working from only one side of your brain.** Effective salespeople understand that they must force themselves to become Mentally Ambidextrous.

Your job as a salesperson is to quickly figure out which lobe your customer works from. Then, you must communicate with that side of their brain.

In my experience, **most salespeople tend to be right-brainers.** They are dreamers, easily able to see the potential in a good idea. They play from their hearts. So as a right-brain salesperson you will be most comfortable working with a right-brain client. Spend plenty of time building rapport. Use your setup period to discuss your families, sports, and even ambitions for the future. Build relationship. Help your right-brain friend understand the "experience" your product offers. Detail the benefits in a personal and human manner. Help him see the big picture in a way that he can appreciate.

If, on the other hand, **your customer is a left-brainer**, she will need more data. She may not be as interested in a personal relationship as her right-brain peers. With such an individual spend less time talking about colors and esthetics. Focus on the details. Bring stats and statistics. Show the quantifiable benefits of your product. Discuss bottom-line benefits. And, don't expect a sale based on emotions.

With years of experience under my belt, I'm convinced that the best use of your time with a client is to figure out which brain lobe he or she operates from...then communicate that way.

As you learn the art of determining lobe preference, your closing rate will climb and you will learn to love the process.

LEFT   **RIGHT**

THOUGHT SPARKLER 4

The Myth of the 40-Hour Work Week

In the 1930's the United States government told us a lie. They told us that if we were working 40 hours per week…we were fully employed. Wow. That may have been the first time in 5000 years of recorded human history that anyone had ever heard that! Historically, a typical workweek included 12-hour days, six days a week.

There are 168 hours in a week. As a guy who has worked plenty of 80- and 90-hour weeks, I can tell you **there's nothing that says you can't work more** than 40 of them. As a matter of fact, some of the most successful people I know are people who work half-time…12-hour days.

Seriously, if you just want to get by and retire at 70 with Social Security, 40 hours per week might do it. But if you dream of living an extraordinary life, you may want to work more. You will find joy in your work. It won't be a burden.

Great salespeople are the ones who **pay no attention to the clock**. As a matter of fact, they see the clock as their friend. They realize that most of their peers are clock-watchers who can't leave work early enough. But fabulously effective salespeople thrive on working when their peers are goofing off. They see it as an opportunity to get ahead. The good news is you don't have to be smart, highly educated, or well connected to work some extra hours.

Some people will protest and say, "If I work more than 40 hours every week I won't have time with my family and friends."

In a word: **WRONG!** Don't fall for the line that you can't have a life if you work more than 40 hours each week.

You can. It is simply a matter of managing your time. Think about it. Do a little personal inventory of what you're doing with your time. Suppose you decided to routinely invest 60 hours weekly in your work. Then factor in some sleep time. Since much of the American workforce is desperately sleep-deprived, be sure you get enough...say eight hours nightly. That's another 56 hours. We're now up to 116 of our 168 hours. Now, let's include some time for personal stuff, meals, church, grooming, etc. Let's say 18 hours weekly. We're now up to a 134 hours. By my count, that leaves you with 34 hours. And if we turned off the TV, quit wasting time, and stopped indulging in too much recreation, we could do a lot of good things.

Research in 2007 reported that the average father spends 6.5 hours weekly with his children. (By the way, that's up 153 percent since the 1960s.) But let's suppose you want to be a great parent and you elect to spend twice as much time with your kids...13 hours weekly. You'd still have 21 more hours to do with as you wish.

But sadly, the black hole for many of us isn't the time we spend at work or with our families. It's the time we spend in front of the tube. Research says that the average American watches 35 hours of television each week! Unbelievable!

No, I'm not suggesting that you can't allow some time for TV and video games. But remember, one of the main reasons we watch all the TV and play all those video games is because we're in a mental funk. We

feel depressed. So, just like a junkie, we "shoot up" by numbing our brains this way. It gives us a temporary release and distracts our sadness.

So, it would be fair to ask, "Where does this funk come from?"

For many of us it comes from concerns about not having enough money. Sometimes it's because we're disappointed in our own failures and lack of productivity. Other times it's because we realize that our peers are performing better than we are.

So, here's my question to you: which one of those problems would not be solved (and, resolved) if you simply spent more time in productive selling? The selling will lighten your money concerns. The selling will give you a sense of dignity, accomplishment, and self-worth. And the selling will make you stand taller with your peers.

People who work more hours become more productive in all their activities. The time they spend with their families is more focused and gratifying. The time they spend serving others and nurturing their spiritual lives is more fulfilling. And the time they spend watching TV is more enjoyable…and less guilt-ridden.

The fact is: laziness and diligence have one thing in common. They are both self-fulfilling prophecies. Whichever way you choose to spend your life will be fulfilled in the way your life ends up. Choose carefully.

A FINAL WARNING: As a speaker and writer I have to paint with a broad brush. Most of what I say will apply to most people. But there are always those for whom my advice is not appropriate. If you tend to be a workaholic, disregard what I've said in this Thought Sparkler. Your job is to rebalance your life in the other direction. I don't encourage anyone to work as many hours as I once did. Routinely working 80- and 90-hour weeks is crazy. It's dangerous. It can break your health physically, relationally, and spiritually. Beware!

STEVE'S TIMELY REMINDERS

THE **GREATEST SALESPEOPLE**

DO THE **right thing**.

NOT because it's the *easiest thing* to do. **NOT** because it's necessarily the **Most Profitable Thing** to do. THEY DO THE RIGHT THING **because** IT'S THE RIGHT THING TO DO...

and they put value in that.

THOUGHT SPARKLER 5

GREAT SALESPEOPLE USE
"CANNED" PRESENTATIONS!

As I mentioned earlier in this book, one of the most important summers of my life was the summer I spent selling books for the Southwestern Company in Nashville. The first week of the summer, before sending us to points all over several states, was sales school.

Wow, I learned a lot!

And was there ever a lot of homework. Each night, after classes when we returned to our motel, the company expected us to spend the evenings committing our sales talks to memory. We were told to read, reread, and rehearse our talks with our fellow students. The Southwestern managers told us our job was simple: be dumb enough to do as we were told. They warned us that failed salespeople were the ones who thought they were smarter than the company. These were the ones who felt no need to memorize the sales talks. Instead they did their own thing. They improvised. They thought they were smarter than the pros who had spent hundreds of hours selling, learning, conceiving, and writing the sales talks.

Curiously, the "smart" salespeople typically sold fewer books, made less money, and washed out more often than those of us who were "dumb" enough to memorize our presentations.

ONE BEST WAY

In fact, there is always only one best way to do anything. There may be fifty ways to accomplish a goal…but there remains one way that works best. Successful people are those people who find the best way to do something and simply replicate it over and over and over and over and over again.

Over the years I've sold millions of dollars of products and services by simply repeating the same sales presentations over and over again. I tend to use the same presentation for the same product every time. Granted, over time I learn better phrases and points. When this happens I incorporate them into my sales talks. But these decisions are made thoughtfully and deliberately.

What the Beach Boys Taught Me About "Canned" Presentations

In case you're not 200 years old, allow me to tell you about the Beach Boys.

The Beach Boys began their American pop music ascendance in the early 1960s when they released their first tunes on the sandy beaches of Southern California. And like they say, the rest is history. With scores of hit records, thousands of concerts, and successful television appearances, many music historians consider the Beach Boys to be one of the most important American rock groups ever. Today, over 55 years later, they're still making music and filling concert halls.

A while back I had an opportunity to visit with Al Jardine, one of the Beach Boys' earliest members. As we talked, I asked him what it was about the Beach Boys that had allowed them to last on a multi-generational level. His answer was both simple and profound. He told me that the Beach Boys weren't in the business of singing songs. They were in the business of building moods.

My wife Bonnie and I have attended several Beach Boy concerts. I've always been impressed by how these guys are able to come out and sing the same songs they've sung thousands of times for decades and keep audiences in the palms of their hands.

Some years ago it hit me. The Beach Boys have a canned presentation. They don't reinvent the wheel with every show. They sing the same songs and tell the same jokes. But, they are so good at it…it never sounds canned.

THE COMPLAINT

Some will complain, "I don't like canned presentations because they sound canned. The fact is, if it sounds canned…it ain't!

Once a presentation is truly canned it will sound fresh and invigorating every time you share it with a client. It will illuminate the product, pre-answer many of the predictable objections, and leave your client fully informed.

After all, we can food to keep it fresh. Why not do the same with our sales presentations?

THOUGHT
SPARKLER

6

KICK UP SOME DUST...PROSPECT!

No matter what you read in the latest book, *How to Get Rich Selling Your Stuff Without Doing Any Work*, prospecting is still the mother's milk of a sales career. There is no substitution. Without prospecting there will be no prospects. Without prospects there will be no demonstrations. Without demonstrations there will be no closes. Without closes there will be no commissions.

But prospecting comes hard for many salespeople. It has been estimated that over seventy percent of sales professionals consider it their leading challenge. The worst cure for a sales slump? The afternoon matinee.

THE BEST CURE FOR A SALES SLUMP? KICK UP SOME DUST BY PROSPECTING.

Over the years I've learned that the best thing to do when business is slow...is to kick up some dust! Following are eight strategies that you may find helpful.

1. PROSPECT WITH VOICE MAIL. I like voice mail. It allows me to say what I want to say without being contradicted.

So here's an idea: Start your morning with voice mails. Simply call six people you'd like to visit and leave a short message like, "Hi, my name is Steve Diggs and I was hoping to borrow four minutes of your time today to share an idea that you may find interesting. I'll try to reach you (or, drop by) around 10:50."

By the way, I suggest making these calls early. The sweet spot is probably around 7:00 to 8:15 am. This way you're less likely to reach the person...but they can tell that you are an early riser and serious about business. Also, if he does pick up the phone, he's more likely to give you a few minutes of his time before the day starts.

2. TAKE THE ELEVATOR. A fun place to prospect is on elevators. Think about it: a captive audience. Simply be the last person to get on the elevator. Then, when the doors close watch everyone else turn around to face the doors. Everyone, that is, except you. As you face the crowd...smile, pull out your business cards, and say something like, "The reason I called you all here today is to introduce myself. I'm in the business of (whatever) and I would be happy to visit further with any of you who would like to do so."

Not everyone can pull this one off...but maybe you can.

3. Start at the top of a tall building with a handful of business cards and work your way down. Go into any office that might need what you're selling. Be prepared not to meet the boss. You're likely not to get past the receptionist. Don't begin by asking to see the top dog. Instead, spend a warm moment with the person in front of you. Then, before leaving simply ask, "Could you take a moment and introduce me to your boss before I leave?"

Of course, as with all my ideas, be sure that this is permitted before you do it.

4. Be a giver of gifts. Over the years I've found that giving thoughtful gifts is a wonderful way to, as Dale Carnegie once said, "Make friends and influence people."

49

As a 22-year-old real estate agent, I quickly learned how hard it was to compete with seasoned pros who knew all the tricks, the city fathers, and were connected with all the decisions makers.

Since I didn't have those connections, many of my days were spent knocking on "For Sale By Owner" doors. This was a time when most women stayed home and cared for their families. Most of these ladies were happy to take my card, but said they would not hire me until I'd also met with their husbands. To my chagrin, I noticed that my business card frequently was added to a growing stack of cards from other agents.

That's when I had my big idea. I'd build my business by giving away roses. In the morning I would stop at the florist and pick up a bunch of boxed, single, long-stemmed roses. Then, as I visited with the ladies, I left them a card and a rose. Suddenly, they liked me and were happy for me to come back in the evening. (Also, I found that some husbands were curious to

see who was giving roses to their wives.) Bottom line...this strategy became a fabulous listing tool!

Today things have changed. But people still like gifts. One of my favorite things to do is go by the donut shop, buy several boxes of donuts...and drop them off to clients and prospects. **I call this Krispy Kreme Diplomacy.** Boy, does it leave a good taste in their mouths. (Pun intended.)

5. Consider writing a book. I say this realizing that this strategy is only appropriate for a small percentage of salespeople. But you might be one of them.

In 1990 I published my first book, *Putting Your Best Foot Forward*. The book was about what my ad agency work had taught me about small

51

business advertising. I was fortunate enough to have a publisher who paid the expenses and handled national distribution. But I decided to purchase a couple thousand copies for myself. Then I thought, "How am I going to sell these?!"

The fact is, I didn't sell very many. Finally with stacks of boxed books in my way, I began giving them away to prospects and encouraging my account managers to do the same. Soon we realized that this was one of the best marketing tools we'd ever run across!

The downsides of writing a book are obvious. Writing is time consuming. (Don't I know that!) And since you will likely be self-publishing, it's going to cost some money. However, with new production techniques and on-demand printing, books are far less expensive to produce than they used to be.

But the upsides are there, too.

- Your book will position you as an expert. It builds your credibility.
- A book is a real gift as it has a high perceived value.
- It's a very personal item to share with others.
- A book is like a business card on steroids! It is rarely thrown out. It sits out in full view of others...complete with your name and topic.

6. BECOME A PROSPECT GIVER. Be as concerned for other salespeople as you are for yourself. When you find an individual who could use the product another salesperson sells...put them together. In many cases that other salesperson will return the favor. And, even if she doesn't, you'll feel good about what you've done.

7. MAKE THE WEB WORK FOR YOU. Whenever feasible, before you call on a prospect, take a couple of minutes to do a Google, Facebook, LinkedIn, Twitter, or other online search. In less than five minutes you can get a wealth of info. Check his proper title, interests, past employers, etc. This will personalize and fast-forward your conversation.

8. ASK FOR REFERRALS. When you have a satisfied customer, ask for one or two names of other people he thinks might be interested in your product. This gives you a wonderful opening when you contact that person: "My friend and client, Pat Daniels, encouraged me to touch base with you. He's found my service very helpful and thought you might also. Can we visit for a few minutes?"

I know. I can hear you right now, "Steve, does this stuff really work?" The answer is: Nope. These ideas don't always work. But they do sometimes.

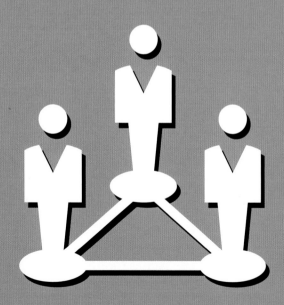

STEVE'S ~TIMELY~ REMINDERS

SUCCESS only happens when your **DREAMS** overwhelm your **FEARS**!

Qualify. Qualify. Qualify!

The most effective salespeople spend a big percentage of their time qualifying their prospects. If you don't take shortcuts on this…you will have a much better selling career. But in fact, most salespeople are so glad to have someone who will listen to them…they'll pitch their product or service to anyone. Huge mistake.

Remember that your most valuable commodity is time. And there's a finite amount of it. 168 hours weekly. No more. No less. The question is: how will you use your time?

Often people who are new to selling confuse two very different things: talking to folks about their product…and being a salesperson. Sitting around talking to someone doesn't make you a salesperson. It makes you a professional visitor!

This is why the best salespeople focus first on qualifying their prospects. Professionals don't waste time trying to sell steaks to vegetarians. It's not about talking someone into buying a product she doesn't need or want. It's not about pushing your service on people who really can't afford it. Just because someone closes lots of deals doesn't mean that he's a great salesman.

The key is finding the right person with a real need for your product

How Does This Work?
A person becomes great at qualifying by doing three things:

1) **ASKING.** The best salespeople are the best question askers. Spend plenty of time learning about your prospect's true interests and needs. Probe. Ask follow up questions. Focus on your prospect…not the commission you hope to earn.

2) **LISTEN.** Experts tell us that only seven percent of our communication is verbal. Much of the rest is receiving…or listening. As I've said before, God gave us one mouth and two ears. Maybe that's a good ratio for how much talking vs. listening we should do.

3) **REPHRASE.** Restate. Reframe. When your prospect has shared her needs, interests, and feelings with you: rephrase, restate, and reframe what you think you have heard.

"Did I hear you correctly when you said such and such?"

If she says, "Yes," you're heading in the right direction.

A HARD TRUTH

I know how it feels to need to make a sale. Sometimes we're tempted to take shortcuts and not put the prospect first. I guess all salespeople have done this at some point. I certainly have. And, I'm not proud of it. But I've repented of those sins and I strive to do better with each new day.

The hard truth is, not everyone you meet is going to be a good prospect. It's your job to sort them out. Make careful and selfless decisions. When you make up your mind to do things the right way, I believe you'll find:

• The people who prove to be legitimate prospects will be far easier to sell to.
• You won't waste nearly as much time.
• Your sales efforts will be far more productive and profitable.
• You'll sleep better at night

Thought Sparkler

8

STEVE'S KILLER CLOSES...
ASKING THE RIGHT QUESTIONS

I'm about to arm you with a machine gun, so I want to begin with a warning. I always hesitate discussing closing techniques until I'm sure that I'm not arming a sales terrorist. The techniques I'm about to share with you will help you make sales. That can be a good or a bad thing. It's a good thing if you use these closes thoughtfully and with a desire to serve your clients' actual needs. But these closes can be bad if used for self-interest.

Also, I differ with sales managers who teach young salespeople to,

"Close, Close, Close!"

Such managers are short sighted. In some cases they're getting pressure from above to hit the numbers. In other cases they're simply feathering their own nests. Some sales forces work on a plan that expects high turnover and they simply want a person to sell until they burnout or get fed up. In an earlier time, some car dealers did just this. They would hire just about anyone hoping they would stick around long enough to sell some cars to their friends and families. Then, if they left—so what? There were always more where they came from.

This is not how a great sales career is built.

This is why I don't believe in closing at all costs. Actually closing should only be done when you have a fully qualified prospect. Assessed his needs. And you are fully confident that your product or service is a good fit and can be of true benefit. Remember, there are lots of fish in the sea. Sometimes it's best to cut bait and find another fishing spot.

Great selling boils down to asking the right questions…and doing a lot of listening.

Here are 14 of MY FAVORITE CLOSES and CLOSING QUESTIONS

Not every one of these will fit your personality. That's okay. There are plenty to choose from. Most of these are not original with me. But they are all time tested. They work.

Frankly, I don't know the source of most of them. But where I do, I've given the appropriate credit. The titles you see are, in some cases, my own and in other cases they're titles used by others.

My hope is that you will find a few that you like best. Commit them to memory. And, as I said earlier, practice them over and over. Then "can" them…so well they don't sound "canned."

1. THE "COMPROMISE" CLOSE. When you have come to the last moment of the presentation but your buyer is holding out with a single objection that you have the ability to eliminate, a great question is simply, "If I can do that for you today, will you okay the purchase?" (Note, that I prefer the phrase, "okay the purchase," instead of, "sign the contract.")

This is a good close, because it both solves the problem and helps you determine whether the buyer's objection is real, or simply an excuse for not buying.

2. THE "WERE YOU SINCERE?" CLOSE. There will be occasions when you'll get the sense that you're being strung along by the buyer…but you aren't totally sure. You don't want to say, "Were you telling me the truth or were you lying when you said you wanted to buy this?" A simple closing question that has helped me is to ask, "Were you sincere when you said that you wanted this product (or, that you had the power to make a decision, etc.)?" This will put the pressure on the prospect to fess up. They either have to say yes, or begin making excuses. If they do the latter, I generally excuse myself for greener pastures.

3. THE "CONSULTATIVE" CLOSE. A good way to gauge the prospect's interest level is to ask, "Are we tracking so far? Do you feel like this product is what you need?" If she says, yes. Great! Pull out the contract. But if she hesitates or says no, your response is, "Why not?" Then listen closely. You're about to get a good temperature reading on where she's at in the process. You will either need to discuss the matter further, or boogie out the door.

4. THE "QUESTION THE BUYER'S QUESTIONS" CLOSE.
If the buyer asks, "Is it available with a grey finish?" You might respond by saying, "Would you like it in a grey finish?" Then listen carefully as your prospect's response may help you gauge their true level of interest.

5. THE "TIME IS OF THE ESSENCE" CLOSE. Warning: Never, never use this close unless it's absolutely the truth. But once in a while, you'll have a situation where you know the prospect needs and wants your service…but he simply can't seem to make a decision…and seems to see no urgency. If there is a sale that ends at the end of the month, or if the shelf life is about to expire, or if the schedule is almost full; try this, "I know you want this product. And, I know we've agreed that it will do the job you need done. But Jason, remember this is a model closeout. We only have nine units left. And the company's ending the sale in six days. You're not going to improve on this price. Why not throw your leg over the bar and we'll do the deal."

6. THE "ASSUMPTIVE" CLOSE. Although this is a close that is frequently misused by high-pressure salespeople, it does serve a wonderful purpose in certain situations. On occasions when you're working with a prospect that seems to be holding himself back, this is a close that may help him along. Simply recap what you've discussed up to this point. "So far we have agreed that this policy covers the items that you have been concerned about. And, we've agreed that the price is within your range. And you've learned a lot about our company's history and financial strength. So, we can go ahead and begin the process. Okay?"

7. THE "YOU DO THE MATH" CLOSE. This is one of mine and I like it. As a matter of fact, I used this close just today. Often buyers (myself included) become overly focused on the short-term cost rather than the long-term benefits of a product. If you're dealing with such a client, try this, "Joe, I know this has a big front-end expenditure, but let's remember the long-term benefits. This is the highest quality product in its category. Yes, it costs more than the others…about 50 percent more. But, it's guaranteed to last for at least seven years. All of the studies conclude that the competitors' similar products last less than three years. You do the math."

8. "THE "I'LL THROW IN A FREEBIE" CLOSE. Everyone likes a good deal. We all like to get a gift. So why not give one to your buyer? Whether it comes out of your commission or the boss's pocket…this close really makes sense…and it works! When you know your prospect is within a hair's breadth of either okaying the deal or walking away…why risk it? Why not throw in a freebie? But make sure that the gift is predicated on her buying. Also be sure that it will enhance the product you're

selling. In other words, don't give her a free magazine subscription unless you're selling magazines. If you're selling a computer, give away some free software. If you're selling a car, throw in some free oil changes and car washes. I frequently offer a free breakout session when someone is considering me for a keynote.

9. THE "REVERSE" CLOSE. Unlike the Assumptive Close above, the Reverse Close is for prospects who enjoy making salespeople squirm. So instead of assuming that he wants to buy your product, ask, "Is there any reason that would keep you from making a decision on this today?" If he says no, chances are…you're about to make a sale!

10. THE "REDUCTION TO THE RIDICULOUS" CLOSE. Sometimes a customer simply needs to understand the long-term nature of your product. When she complains about the price, say, "Yes, it's going to cost some money…you're right. So let's look at this. The price is $500. But you will be using it for more than four years. When I divide $500 by 1000 days (the number of business days in four year years) that comes out to 50 cents per day. Is that too much to pay?"

11. THE "CLOSED-END" CLOSE. This one is tricky. But sometimes it works well. After you've fully discussed all the details (features, warranties, price, etc.) and you sense that your prospect is open and ready to buy, ask, "Sara, are you ready to let me begin the process?" If she says yes…whoopee!

12. THE "WOULD YOU LIKE MY HELP?" CLOSE. This is a close discussed in Baseline Selling by Dave Kurlan. I like it because it's friendly, compassionate, and to the point. Also, it helps you remain in the position of a trusted advisor instead of just another salesman.

13. THE "WORKING BACKWARDS" CLOSE. This is an especially good close for people who have a hard time making a decision but are on a timeline. Simply say, "Pat, you told me you had to have this print job in the mail by the 15th of next month. That's only 20 days from now. Whomever you get to print this is going to have to order the stock and do the prepress work. Then, you will have to go over the proofs. After that it has to go to press. Then, it will have to go through the liquid lamination process and the pages will have to be perfect bound and 3-knife cut. After that, it will have to be fabricated and boxed. Then sent to the postal service." Believe me, this close has helped get a lot of buyers off the dime!

14. THE "COLUMBO" CLOSE. Do you remember the old Columbo show? It was a whodunit starring Peter Falk as an LAPD homicide detective with his own way of solving crimes. He would frequently conclude an interview with a suspect and turn and walk away. But with the tension now broken, he would turn on his heels and walk back in and say, "Just one more thing…" He always followed that up with a comment or question that was riveting…and frequently broke the case. You can do the same thing. Have a preplanned comment or question. Then as you're leaving the prospect's office literally turn around on your heels, walk back in, and say, "Let me share one final thought with you…"

FINAL THOUGHTS

Keep your focus. Be sure that everything you do is for the benefit of your prospect. Good closing seeks to solve a very real problem or need in the prospect's life.

Remember that listening is your most important tool. After you've made your presentation and done a close, shut up. Wait for a response. Feel no responsibility to fill the void. The long silence can help both of you collect your thoughts. Wait. Don't say another word until your client speaks.

STEVE'S TIMELY REMINDERS

There comes a **TIME** to get

past your past.

Remember that **PAST DUMB**

does not equal **FUTURE DUMB**.

It's *NEVER TOO LATE* to begin doing

the right thing.

Your job? **Make the next right**

decision.

THOUGHT SPARKLER 9

MY ALL-TIME **FAVORITE** CLOSE

In the next few lines I'm going to share with you my most favorite and, probably, most effective close. But to call this a close doesn't do it justice. In fact this close actually begins at the very beginning of the presentation…from the rapport building to the setup to the demonstration.

As I mentioned in the last Thought Sparkler, it's way past time for our profession to drive a stake in the heart of old-school selling that admonished, "Close, close, close… at all costs!" In that environment salespeople routinely belittled customers behind their backs. They saw selling as an adversarial relationship. Granted, sometimes it got sales. But this was a time when buyers were far less sophisticated. They had fewer options. And, there was no Internet.

In those days salespeople were trained to ignore objections. Simply keep going and pretend you didn't hear what the prospect had just said. Some trainers taught young salespeople to ignore the objection until the prospect had repeated it three or four or more times. All in all, it was a pretty scuzzy way to treat people. But it worked…sometimes.

No doubt there are still some of those old dinosaurs roaming the earth. But today, good sales training focuses on showing prospects honor and respect. The goal is for both sides to leave smiling.

That's why I like this close so much. **I call it Pre-Answering.**

I have found that the best way to avoid interruptive questions during a presentation, and needless objections at the end of the presentation, is to begin the presentation by

Pre-Answering them. Yep. I know that's vastly different even from what many trainers will tell you…but, for me, it works.

To use Pre-Answering effectively there are several things I like to do before meeting with the prospect:

1. First, I think about that specific client. His likes and dislikes. Her nature. Is she lighthearted and easygoing or tightly wound? Does he like for me to paint word pictures and discuss features or just cut to the chase?

2. Next, I pre-act by thinking about what this specific client is likely to object to. If his company is losing money, he will likely object to the cost. If they are always on horrible deadlines, I need to plan an early delivery date. If they have had bad experiences with salespeople in the past, I need to distinguish myself from the other guys.

3. Then, I plan responses for those objections…not to use at the end of my presentation…but to use at the very beginning and throughout. For the budget-conscious prospect I might begin by saying, "I realize that we're in a slow market climate and business has been slower than usual, so that's why I've developed a price structure that I believe you'll find appealing and very doable." This keeps my prospect from either interrupting and throwing the presentation off track, or sitting silently thinking about his concerns.

4. Finally, before I visit with my prospect…I practice. That's why they make mirrors—to PRACTICE! Work on your Pre-Answers and be certain that they all make sense. Then, go and make your pitch!

REMEMBER that the goal is to bring the final close in on a smooth and easy glide path unencumbered by a lot of negative concerns at the end.

You always want to conclude on an **upbeat note**.

Try this...I think you'll find it helpful.

NEGOTIATING: THE ART OF GETTING THE GREEN LIGHT!

Selling and negotiating go together like ugly on a frog. The two are first cousins. Rarely does a salesperson get exactly what he wants. Virtually all closes end up with a negotiated agreement. The greatest salespeople learn to live well on half loaves.

So, it behooves you to learn how to negotiate, because your prospect is set and ready to negotiate with you. In one study, more than 65 percent of respondents said they had tried to negotiate with sellers. And, among that group, more than 85 percent had successfully negotiated a better price.

But many salespeople have a warped idea of what negotiating is all about. They hate the thought of negotiating. When the word comes up, it's typical to hear comments like,

- "I don't want to be confrontational."
- "I'm not a manipulative sort of a person."
- "I don't want to beat anything out of another person."
- "I can't lie with a straight face."

WHAT NEGOTIATING IS NOT

If the thought of negotiating makes you queasy, rest easy, my friend. I want to show you some of the benefits of a great negotiation. But before we delve too deeply into this, I want you to understand four things good negotiating is not:

1. Good negotiations are not confrontational. A good negotiation can, and should, be handled with dignity and respect.

2. Good negotiations are not manipulative. Successful negotiating sets up a win-win atmosphere where both parties come out ahead. The goal should always be to help everyone involved get what he or she wants.

3. Good negotiations are not dishonest. Good negotiators do not tells lies to gain the advantage; they tell the truth.

4. Good negotiations are not emotionally painful. Negotiating should be fun for both parties.

14 Secrets of the Great Negotiators

When you read through these, you may say to yourself, "Well, that was obvious." That's because many of these suggestions are rooted in common sense and the idea of treating other people the way you would want them to treat you.

1. Use time to your advantage. Try to negotiate when you have plenty of time. The less rushed you are, the better. Your buyer can tell when you're more anxious to sell than she is to buy. Avoid this temptation. Take your time. Be patient. Usually the less emotion you invest in a negotiation, the better.

2. Figure out what your prospect wants out of the deal.
This isn't always obvious. Frequently the prospect doesn't tell you what he really wants to accomplish. The old saying that, "Buyers are liars," is too harsh. I prefer to think that prospects frequently haven't processed their own thoughts and goals fully. It's your job to help them do so.

3. Get into the other person's skin. Always try to look at the deal from her side of the fence. This will help you craft benefit-oriented comments. You won't accidently say something offensive. Sincerely try to structure a transaction that's as good for her as it is for you.

4. Leave the other person with a graceful way of escape.

Most people think negotiating is the art of winning arguments. Not true! If your negotiation becomes an argument—you've already lost!

One of the best ways to leave the other person a graceful way out is to avoid putting him in a corner in the first place. For instance, instead of telling him how much it costs, begin by asking him how much he would like to pay. Here's why: If you begin the negotiation process by telling him how much he'll have to pay, he will likely push back with a lower number. At that point, you're left with three unappealing options:

1. **You could accept his price.**
2. **You could pass on the deal.**
3. **You could ask him to increase what's he is willing to pay.**

At first impulse, the third option (asking him to increase what he's willing to pay) may not seem so bad. But it could be a real deal breaker. The minute you ask for more money, you infer that his first number was ill-considered. He may feel offended and become defensive. That's definitely not the desired response!

5. Never be discourteous or condescending. It's normal to have
some frustration with a client who belittles you, shows up late, or behaves badly.   In most cases this has far more to do with their own flaws and insecurities than it has to do with you. You will sometimes be tempted to behave the same way. This is always a bad decision. You need to bite your tongue and hold back the glib comments. Sarcasm is a characteristic that you can't afford. You may win the battle but you'll lose the war. Remember: Never get into a puking contest with a buzzard!

6. Employ your best ally: Knowledge. Never go into any important negotiation without doing your homework. One of the first rules of being a lawyer is to never ask a question which you don't already know the answer. The same holds true for good negotiators. A little "pregame" research can pay huge dividends. Learn all you can about your buyer. Study the competition. Do a Google search. Be prepared to conduct an informed conversation.

7. Remember: Negotiation is a process...not a battle. Take your time. Be at peace. Go into a negotiation with good will and true empathy for the other party. Try to win a friend first.

8. Become a good communicator. Learn to use words clearly and precisely. Speak loudly enough to be heard. Avoid using technical or professional jargon that may confuse the other party or make her feel patronized. Stay focused. If you're going to make a lengthy presentation, practice it in the mirror first.

9. Get to the decision maker. One of the things I used to teach account executives at my ad agency was that a presentation for a new account would probably not succeed if they weren't talking to the person who could make a final decision. Nothing is more frustrating than to make a full-blown pitch, only to realize your prospect has no authority to "green light" the project. Before you start the conversation, ask, "If we reach a mutually agreeable price, can you give the final okay?" If the person says no, then try to go up line as far as you must to get to that all-important decision maker.

10. Remain focused—don't bring other problems or issues into the negotiation. Forget about peripheral issues that might cloud the negotiating process. Stay on message. I would even encourage you to check your emotions at the door. If you begin to act on your emotions (such as anger, fear, excitement), you may be facing failure. During negotiations, think with your head and not your heart.

11. Check your body language. People "listen" to more than just your words—they also "listen" to your body. As I've said, our words make up only part of the message we send to others. Other things, such as our tone, facial movements, and body language, can send a message that's completely opposite from the words coming out of our mouths. When negotiating, use friendly, inviting gestures. Lean forward. Smile easily. Be open.

12. Stay calm. Ignore personal insults—that's not why you're here. If the other person gets ugly or emotional, be kind in return. This is absolutely the time to be turning the other cheek. I prefer to assume that a negative response from someone stems from his or her own fear of negotiating. A kind, gentle, nonthreatening response to even the most vicious comment can save both the deal and your own dignity. In the course of a sales career you will have a lot of customers complaining about a lot of stuff. This is actually a good thing. Think about it. If your profession didn't come with some significant challenges it would be so easy that everybody and his brother would become salespeople. Then, with everyone selling...who'd be left to buy? When someone knocks your product don't take it personally. They hate what you're selling...not you. And besides, if they are unkind to you, trying to get even is a losing battle. As the late Zig Ziglar said, "You need to decide whether you're going to feed your ego...or feed your family."

13. If the other person reneges, don't panic or become angry. Sometimes a person will get nervous and try to back out of a deal. Don't respond emotionally. Slow down, take a breath, and be gentle. As I mentioned in the closing section, one phrase that has helped me in such cases is to simply look the other person in the eye and kindly ask, "Were you sincere when you agreed to purchase this item at this price?" Now, he must either honor his earlier commitment, clarify a misunderstanding he may have had, or admit he isn't going to live up to his word.

14. Enter a negotiation with one or two alternative plans.

By doing some pre-negotiation thinking, you'll be able to anticipate the most likely objections to your presentation. Be prepared. Always have a Plan B and C.

STEVE'S TIMELY REMINDERS

MONEY is the outgrowth of successful selling. But money DOESN'T MAKE ONE SUCCESSFUL. It's only when we learn to SHARE with others...and see the BLESSINGS that come to others...that we begin to experience *TRUE SUCCESS*.

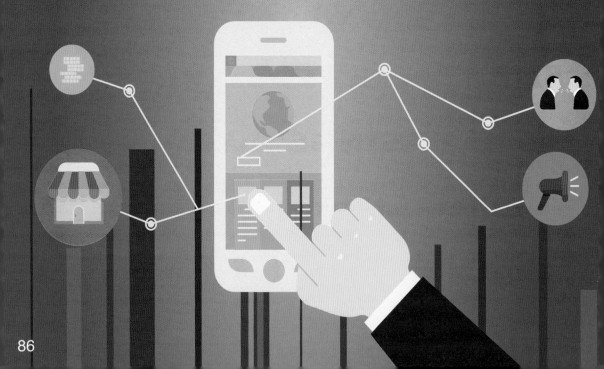

THOUGHT SPARKLER
11

AVOID THE CURSE OF TOO MUCH KNOWLEDGE

Over the years I've seen a fistful of business deals and product sales pitches fail because of too much knowledge. "But, Steve," you protest, "didn't you tell me that I need lots of product knowledge?" Yes, I did. But here I'm discussing something a bit different. Let me explain.

Back in my ad agency days I frequently counseled clients to reduce the amount of information they wanted us to communicate to their target audiences. The problem was simple. The clients had spent a lifetime building their company. They knew everything about the business and their product line. And they wanted everyone else to know their story. They failed to realize that their target market was made up of people who were worried about their children, concerned about their jobs, and troubled with their marriages. Additionally, those same people are constantly being bombarded with other advertisers' messages. It's been suggested that the average American is likely exposed to over 2000 marketing messages every day. And when you consider the billboards, radio and TV spots, print ads, names on ballpoint pens, Internet pitches, and product labels—this may be a reasonable number.

So what most people do is tune it all out. They have put up "pre-attentive barriers" to screen out all the clutter.

It follows that the messages that really do get heard must be very special. In advertising, we know that several things help accomplish this:

• Being different than the other guys grabs attention.

• Keeping it simple is vital. Most people don't want more mental strain. The old acrostic still holds: KISS…Keep It Simple Stupid (or, Salesperson).

• Focusing on the benefits to the consumer is paramount. Think about it. Have you ever seen a Coke commercial that talks about how Dr. John Pemberton developed the early formula? Or how many delivery trucks the company owns? Or what their sales projections are? No. And, I doubt you ever will, because Coke understands that customers buy Coke out of self-interest. So Coke associates their products with happy lifestyles. They sell the diet benefits of Diet Coke and Coke Zero. They show how well Coke goes with food.

WHERE THE TERM COMES FROM

The phrase "curse of knowledge" was coined by economists Colin Camerer, George Loewenstein, and Martin Weber. It refers to how some leaders, teachers, and communicators forget where they came from and fail to communicate effectively with their protégés. As a salesperson this can happen to you, too. It's easy to become so engrossed in the product or service you're selling…that you leave your prospect behind.

I would encourage you, in the strongest terms, to avoid three sales killers:

1. Industry jargon.

2. Fast talk.

3. Speaking in shorthand. When you become thoroughly immersed in your company and the products you sell, it's easy to talk to prospects like you do with the sales team at work. Don't do this. Count every sentence you speak and ask, "If I'd never heard of this product would I understand what's being said?"

The operative phrase: Get into your client's shoes before you begin the hike.

THOUGHT SPARKLER 12

IF IT'S WORTH DOING...IT'S WORTH DOING WRONG

Two of the reasons salespeople fail are:

1. The fear of failure.
2. The fear of rejection.

Think about it—how much more successful and joyful would you be if you were totally unafraid of failing and being rejected? These fears cost careers, incomes, and relationships.

But here's the good news: you can do a lot to conquer these fears if you want to. I don't believe it's realistic to try to get rid of all the butterflies in our stomachs… but we can teach those butterflies to fly in formation.

You need to realize that everyone you know is desperately insecure. No one has all the answers. No one wins every game. No salesperson closes every deal.

On balance, most people have about the same intelligence level. Sure, some have more and some have less. But 68 percent of all IQ scores fall between

85 and 115. (Source: Reference.com) And if your IQ is in the 90 to 115 range,

THERE'S NO REASON WHY YOU CAN'T SUCCEED IN THIS BUSINESS.

Granted, it may take you a little longer than someone else...but you can do it. Think back to your school days. Don't you remember a kid in class who had lots of talent yet did very little with it? On the other hand, wasn't there someone who had to pore over her studies hours longer than most...but was toughened by the process and has had a very successful life because of it? The same holds true for many people with physical and health challenges. Frequently the challenges they face toughen their resolve to become maximum performers.

93

It's not always the boldest, brightest, and most bombastic who win the prize. Frequently it's the individual who gets up each morning with no fanfare. Does the right things. Remains a lifelong student of selling. Maintains his priorities and integrity. And determines to help others in the process.

So here's my considered advice: Don't allow your misplaced fears to keep you from stepping into the game.

Don't do stupid stuff. But don't be paralyzed either. Take appropriate chances. Look for innovative ways to do old things. Study when your peers are goofing off. Do something. I would much rather fail while making a gallant effort than fail by doing nothing. Have courage. In most cases the worst your prospect can do is say, "No." And, isn't that where you're already at?

STEVE'S TIMELY REMINDERS

YOU ARE WHAT YOU DO...NOT WHAT YOU SAY YOU WILL DO.

It's time to catch the vision.

MAKE A DECISION. AND, TRAIN THE BUTTERFLIES IN YOUR STOMACH TO FLY IN FORMATION!

STAY HEALTHY

In these final Thought Sparklers, I want to focus on two personal issues that, if properly addressed, will bless your sales efforts many times over. First, we'll look at our health, next we'll zero in on getting control of our money.

Unless you are an Internet genius, a star athlete, or were born to a Fortune 500 CEO, your best way to build wealth is through your sales career. But in order to work, you have to remain healthy.

HERE'S THE SECRET TO A HEALTHY LIFE: CHOOSE YOUR PARENTS CAREFULLY.

But short of that…

The fact is: sick is expensive. I believe we owe it to ourselves and our loved ones to stay healthy. And yes, I'll agree that there are some health issues we cannot avoid. In many cases maladies like cancer and heart disease are hereditary. There's not a lot you can do to prevent someone from T-boning you in an intersection.

On the other hand, many of the injuries and diseases we deal with are self-inflicted. Alcoholism happens when one chooses to drink too much. Some cancers are caused by bad lifestyle choices such as smoking. Sexually transmitted diseases can be caused by promiscuity. Heart disease can come from a lack of self-discipline when we eat badly, don't exercise, and overwork.

WHEN IT ALL CHANGED FOR ME

I was diagnosed with heart disease way back in 1979. They told me to restrict my diet and do regular exercise. But I didn't take it as seriously as I should have. I still overate. I didn't exercise enough. And, I continued working far too many hours. Then it hit. In February 1992, at age 39, I found myself at St. Thomas Hospital in Nashville having five heart bypasses! Whoa!

But in truth, I had earned the honor. I was doing everything wrong.

So I decided to get serious and change some things. I got on a tough diet and lost some real weight. I started working out regularly and strenuously. Today, it's been more than 25 years since my surgery. I haven't eaten a full steak since my bypass. I take a bunch of pills. But I'm still going to the gym. Today, I routinely travel the world: three continents in the last five weeks. I run at full speed. And I feel great! Thank you, Lord!

HERE'S MY POINT

I learned the hard way (which I hope you won't have to) that life is precious. I learned that good health is vital for my work...and my work is the only way I can earn, share, and give to others.

This is why I encourage others to do three things: (NOTE: Of course get your doctor's okay before doing anything that may impact your health.)

1) Get Enough Sleep. As I mentioned earlier, many American adults are sleep-deprived. Experts tell us that a lack of sleep can lead to all sorts of bad stuff: heart disease, some cancers, depression, irritability, and a lack of focus to name a few.

Different people need different amounts of sleep. While a small percentage do okay with four to six hours of sleep per night, many people need seven to eight hours or more. This should be good quality sleep. Unless essential, shut off all of those lights, bells, and beeps on your devices. Get away from the noise. Many people sleep best in a dark room. For some people, a cool room is best. Do what you need to do to sleep tight.

2) Eat Properly. Talk with your doctor or qualified health professional and design a diet that's right for you. Personally, I lean into the Mediterranean-style diet: lots of salmon, olive oil, and fruits and veggies. While it may not be right for everyone, it's worked well for me.

Don't complicate this needlessly. Eat the proper amount of calories. Pay attention to the fats. Watch the 3 Deadly Whites: salt, refined sugar, and flour. In other words, behave yourself.

3) Exercise. Yep, I said it. The bad word. But with all the jokes aside, I'm convinced that exercise is a vital key to good health. Broadly speaking, lots of us have seen real benefit from at least three exercise periods each week. My goal is to, after a warm-up, get my heart rate up to approximately seventy or eighty percent of its capacity, and hold it there for twenty to thirty minutes. Then I do a cool down. Again, get your doc's advice on all of this before you start.

HERE'S THE CHALLENGE

To paraphrase the late Coach Bear Bryant, "The trouble with the road to success is it's filled with too many parking places." Knowing what to do and doing it are very different. Setting goals is the easy part. Sticking to those goals is another thing. But remember, you are a professional salesperson. Your stock in trade is mental toughness. When you see a prize (in this case, good health and the ability to earn), you set a laser focus and go for it. Nothing gets in your way.

THIS IS WHO YOU ARE. THIS IS WHAT YOU DO. YOU CAN DO THIS!

THOUGHT SPARKLER 14
Get Your MONEY Under Control

Over the last 15 years I've spoken to audiences over 1200 times on the topic of personal finance in my *No Debt No Sweat Money Management Seminar*™. I've written scores of articles on the topic and the *No Debt No Sweat*™ book has been a big seller. So it's fair to say that I've got a real interest (and some experience) in the area of money.

THE COLD, HARD FACTS

Today it's typical for a young person to go through twelve years of school and four years of college—supposedly being taught what they need to know to be an educated, productive member of society—without ever being shown how to balance a bank account, do a budget, or avoid a bad credit card deal! The facts are stunning:

- As of this writing, credit card debt nationally is at almost $1 Trillion.
- The average household with credit card debt is carrying a balance of about $15,000. (Source: Debt.org)
- The average monthly car payment is about $500.
- 56 percent of Americans have less than $10,000 saved for retirement. (Money Magazine)

THE CONTRADICTION OF BEING A SALESPERSON

As a salesperson you have an interesting problem. On the one hand, you are in one of the few professions that literally allows you to determine what your income will be. Many sales folks can control their hours on the job, their expenses, their client list, and how hard they work. But on the other hand, many salespeople barely make a survivable living.

A fair question to ask is: Why? Why do people in the selling profession routinely struggle? I believe there are at least two reasons. One, they do too much impulse spending. Two, they tend to have poor money management habits. Let's briefly look at each of these.

SALESPEOPLE TEND TO OVERSPEND FOR SEVERAL REASONS.

This isn't an exhaustive list, but see if you identify with any of these reasons:

• Trying to keep up with the Joneses.

• Trying to impress their clients.

• Because of the uncertain nature of the sales business, many salespeople live too much in the here and now.

• Salespeople tend to be risk takers.

• Because they've had a slow period and they're anesthetizing the pain.

• Because they've had a great month and they're celebrating.

While I've literally written a book on the topic, let me share two brief money control techniques that will greatly reduce your stress and make you a better salesperson.

If You're In Debt Now—GET OUT!
Having no debt feels really good. All the things we buy to help us feel good pale in comparison to the peace we experience when we don't have credit card bills, car payments, or school debt.

So, the question is: How do you get out of debt? I recommend two strategies to get you started: "Steve's 3-Point Steroid Kit" and an aggressive plan of attack.

STEVE'S 3-POINT STEROID KIT

To pay off your debts you're going to need some more money. Here are three important things to do:

1. SELL STUFF. That's right. You're going to sell everything you don't need. This means you keep the wedding photos…but you sell the frames! You're going to have garage sales, post items on eBay…do whatever you have to do. So get busy selling your stuff!

2. CUT EXPENSES. This means we lower our standard of living. When we stop to put $40 of gas in our car—we're not going to put $4 of sodas and chips inside of us! It means we aren't going to the restaurant—we're going home to eat leftovers. It means we're going to stop spending five dollars for 50-cent cups of coffee…period!

3. LEARN HOW TO REALLY WORK. I believe this is the most important of my three steroids. This is when we begin putting in some serious hours selling. I like to encourage salespeople to aim for a 60-hour workweek. And if the collectors are calling, consider even more work hours for a short period of up to a couple of years. You may find these extra work hours are far less painful than the stress of debt. Do a quick review of "Thought Sparkler #5) The Myth of the 40-Hour Work Week."

NOW, GET ROUGH, TOUGH...WITH NO FLUFF...AND KILL THE DEBT!

This is when we look at all of our debts. We make a minimum payment on each debt...except for one of them. This is the one of your choosing that you zero in on determined to murder. You apply the three steroids above and BOOM...you kill that debt. Then you take the money from that paid debt and apply it to your next debt. When that second debt is gone...you go after the third debt, and so on.

By applying these three steroids you'll see your debts melt away even faster. Many people who do this get out of short-term debt within one to four years. You can do this!

2) DO A BUDGET

The only way I know to manage money is to have a written budget. This budget is the lion tamer that's going to get you out of the cage! But as a salesperson you have some unique needs and challenges. Unlike most other people, you probably don't receive equal monthly paychecks. You probably receive varying commissions...and, only when you earn them. And then, there's that feast or famine thing. One month you're broke. The next month you feel rich. And you feel entitled to have some fun after that lean period...right? So you spend all you've earned, and the next month is lean again...and you're broke again. Sound familiar?

So, here's a special approach to budgeting that I teach my sales clients.

1. Begin by determining your total average monthly financial needs.

2. Then, break your back for three or four months and get ahead. Work some 70- and 80-hour weeks. Never spend a dime more than you must. The goal here is to eventually build up the equivalent of one month's expenses. Now, bank it all! This becomes your slush fund.

3. Going forward, never spend more than you've budgeted. If you earn more than is needed…put it into your slush fund. Don't blow it. On those months when you come up short, borrow the needed amount from your slush fund.

This is the way Bonnie and I have lived much of our married lives. And guess what, we haven't had a debt since the 1990. And today we have an abundance. Try it. I think you'll like it!

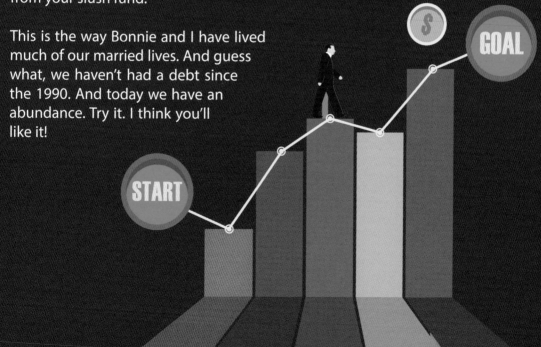

BEFORE WE SAY GOOD-BYE…

Before we say good-bye let me share what's most important to me.

Years ago, I came to a point in life when I realized I didn't have the answers to the most important questions. And, I couldn't fix all the bad things I'd done. I needed a Savior. I learned that salvation and forgiveness are free gifts from God. Also, I learned there was absolutely nothing I could do to earn salvation—it is a free gift from God. The Bible tells us how we can accept this free gift of God's grace:

1. It begins by hearing and believing (or, having faith) that Jesus is who He says He is—the Son of God and our Savior. Romans 10:17 says, "faith comes by hearing the word of God."

2. We must be willing to repent (or, sorrowfully turn away from) our past sins. In Acts 17:30, the Bible says that God "commands all men, everywhere to repent."

3. We need to be willing to confess that Jesus is Lord—the Son of God. "He that confesses me before men, him will I also confess before my father who is in heaven." (Matthew 10:32)

4. Finally, the Bible teaches that we step into Christ through a symbolic burial called baptism. This is when we are immersed in water—allowing our old self to be buried, and arising a new creature in Christ! What a beautiful moment! In Acts 2:38, when a crowd of people asked what they had to do to be saved, the Apostle Peter told them, "Repent and be baptized, every one of you, in the name of Jesus Christ for the forgiveness of your sins. And you will receive the gift of the Holy Spirit."

If you'd like to discuss this further, email me at steve@stevediggs.com.

ABOUT THE AUTHOR

A star salesman himself, STEVE DIGGS (CSP), has been selling…and teaching others how to sell…for over 35 years. From his days with the Southwestern Company to the real estate and automotive businesses, he's done it all. He is the founder of six successful sales-driven companies. Today, his *Fast-Forward Leadership Programs*™ keep Steve's clients on the cutting-edge of industry best practices. Although Steve lives in Nashville, speaking requests take him all over the world. A bestselling author, he has written eleven books and 100's of articles.

Steve is a sought after keynote and breakout speaker, corporate/leadership trainer, C-Suite coach, and thought leader. He is the recipient of the National Speakers Association's Certified Speaking Professional (CSP) designation…the highest earned degree in the speaking industry…held by less than two-percent of speakers worldwide. Steve has shared his insights over 3,000 times on five continents. He is a high-content communications expert who inspires his audiences with wit, storytelling, and an encyclopedic knowledge of leadership strategies, sales, branding and communication skills… always lots of laughs and eye-candy.

Steve and Bonnie were married in 1976. But their love story actually began in February 1972 when, on their first date, Steve told Bonnie that he was going to marry her. Steve says, "So far, so good…she's been picking my option up every year!" Their top priority is serving Jesus and reflecting Him to others. The couple has four grown children and six grandchildren. Home is in Brentwood, Tennessee (a Nashville suburb) where they can be seen traveling the road on their Harley Davidson.

Visit Us At: www.SteveDiggs.com
TO DISCUSS INVITING STEVE TO YOUR NEXT EVENT:
615.300.8263 or steve@SteveDiggs.com

Person to Personal: The People Skills in the Workforce Event™

This is the ultimate team building experience! Designed to accomplish 3 goals by showing your team how to:

- Effectively Relate with Your Customers
- Respond Better to Management
- Play Better in the Sandbox with Each Other

The Come-Back Customer: What Great Companies Do to Keep Them Coming Back™

Steve has helped 100s of companies keep their customers loyal...these are the strategies that will do the same for you!

- Build a Passionate & Enthusiastic Team...with an Eye on the Bottom Line.
- *The Golden 6*™...What You Must Do to Keep a Customer
- The 3 Ways to Make the Customer Experience *MAGIC*!

Building Brand YOU...The Ultimate Challenge™

To compete effectively in today's challenging business climate everyone needs to build a compelling and unforgettable personal brand. Steve will show your organization how to:

- Build Their Personal Brands...to Improve Communication & Sales
- Empower Your Leadership Team to Maximize Market Impact
- Clearly Communicate Their Core Values
- Become Benefit-Oriented People™

The Leadership Summit™

In a world that sends confusing messages about leadership this is a breath of fresh air! Your people will be challenged and encouraged. They will leave renewed, refueled and re-fired...energized with solid biblical reasons to see less tunnel...and more light. Three Sessions:

- The **MIND** of a Leader • The **HEART** of a Leader • The **ATTITUDE** of a Leader

The No Debt No Sweat Personal Money-Management Seminar™

Based on his book of the same name, Steve has presented this seminar over 500 times worldwide. More at www.NDNS.org. Learn how to:

- Kill the Debt Monster & the 9-Keys of Successful Budgeting
- Buy Cars and Insurance the Right Way...and Retire with Dignity
- Build a 7-Step Do-It-Yourseld Credit Repair Kit

PERFECT FOR CHRISTIAN AUDIENCES!